ESCAPE
FROM IRAN

ESCAPE
FROM IRAN

TWO JEWISH GIRLS' STORY OF SURVIVAL

SHIRA YEHUDIT DJALILMAND

MENUCHA PUBLISHERS

Menucha Publishers, Inc.
© 2019 by Menucha Publishers
Designed by Deena Weinberg
Typeset by Rivkah Wolfson
All rights reserved

ISBN 978-1-61465-673-9
Library of Congress Control Number: 2018955122

No part of this publication may be translated, reproduced, stored in a retrieval system, or transmitted in any form or by any means, electronic, mechanical, photocopying, recording, or otherwise, without prior permission in writing from the publisher.

Published and distributed by:
Menucha Publishers, Inc.
1235 38th Street
Brooklyn, NY 11218
Tel/Fax: 718-232-0856
www.menuchapublishers.com
sales@menuchapublishers.com

PHOTO CREDITS
p. 81, 89: Jaap Sanders.
p. 12: Kamyar Adl. p. 13: Xiquinhosilva. p. 14: Alisami. p. 17: Royal Court of Iran. p. 19: Ninara. p. 23: Sajed.ir. p. 25: Bernard Gagnon. p. 26: Author unknown. p. 28: Mammad2002. p. 29: Author unknown. p. 33: Iran Persian Gulf Forever. p. 34: freepik.com. p. 37: Orijentolog. p. 41- Dejan Milinkovic. p. 43: Mahid Mohammadzadeh. p. 45: David Holt. p. 48: Nima Farid. p. 51: Stephan Klage. p. 53: Franek2. p. 56: Gryllida. p. 60: Obaid Raza. p. 63: Koshy Koshy. p. 65: Ehtesham Zahoor. p. 67: Kamil Masood. p. 71: Biba Khan. p. 73: Mawaishasan. p. 74: Syed M. Mohsin Jilani. p. 77: Ziegler175. p. 78: 101holidays.co.uk. p. 84: NoRealNameGiven. p. 87: Greg. p. 93: Swerveut. p. 95: Shoestring. p. 98: Eduard Marmet. p. 100: goisraelgermany. p. 102: Andrew Shiva. p. 104: Ensie and Matthias. p. 105: Someday 1867. p. 107: Arad. End papers: freepik.com

Disclaimer: The events recorded in this book are true, but the exact nature of the conversations and minor episodes were impossible to reconstruct with complete accuracy, due to the passage of time. All the names in this book, with the exception of Jaap Sanders and Mr. Uri Cohen, as well as those of political figures, have been changed for the sake of privacy.

CONTENTS

Acknowledgments 7
Prologue 9

CHAPTER 1: The Calm before the Storm 11
CHAPTER 2: Winds of Change 16
CHAPTER 3: The Revolution 22
CHAPTER 4: Difficult Decisions 27
CHAPTER 5: Secretive Preparations 32
CHAPTER 6: Time to Go 39
CHAPTER 7: Hiding Out 47
CHAPTER 8: Over the Mountains 55
CHAPTER 9: Into the Firing Line 62
CHAPTER 10: Not Safe Yet 69
CHAPTER 11: Refugees in Karachi 76
CHAPTER 12: Bound by Bureaucracy 83
CHAPTER 13: En Route 91
CHAPTER 14: Life in Israel 97

Epilogue	103
Author's Note	109
Timeline of Events	111
Glossary	113

ACKNOWLEDGMENTS

First and foremost, my thanks must go to everyone at Menucha Publishers. To Hirsch and Estie Traube for their broad vision and entrepreneurial spirit, which demonstrates itself in the wonderful variety of fascinating and educational books they bring to the English-speaking Jewish world. To editor-in-chief Esther Heller, whose finely tuned sensitivity takes every book she produces to a higher level. To Chaya Baila Lieber, whose close attention to every detail improved my manuscript immeasurably.

And to all those essential members of the production team without whom this book couldn't happen — editor Cindy Scarr, proofreaders Esther Malky Sonenblick and Daliya Shapiro, graphic artist Rivkah Wolfson, and designer of a stunning front cover, Adina Belsky — thank you all!

Jaap Sanders, the Dutch Jew who helped rescue many Persian Jews, including the girls in this book, was an enormous help to me, not only in finding me my interviewee but also in answering my numerous questions (with infinite patience) about details of the rescue operation.

And, last but not least, thanks to my Persian husband, who was also pestered by infinite questions on every aspect of Jewish life in Iran!

PROLOGUE

Zahedan, Iran, 1987

"The café is just up this side street," said Mr. Hakimian, leading his wife and daughters up a quiet alleyway. "There, you see? Café Dariush, the one with the flowerpot by the door."

Pari and Maheen glanced at each other before they walked in the door. *Here we go*, their glance seemed to say. *There's no turning back now.*

Mr. Hakimian chose a table in the middle of the café. He wanted to make it easy for the smuggler to be able to walk past their table without attracting attention. The café was quiet; Mr. Hakimian didn't know if that was good or bad. If it was quiet, then perhaps no one would notice their meeting. But then maybe people would notice just because it was so quiet.

"What can I get you?" asked the waiter, a sullen, bored-looking youth.

"Oh, er, bring us four sherbets, please," Mr. Hakimian ordered. A delicious sweet, cool sherbet drink would make them all feel better.

The sherbets the waiter brought were surprisingly good. But no one was thinking about sherbet. Everyone was thinking of just one thing: would the smuggler show up?

The time seemed to pass so, so slowly. They tried to make conversation, but no one could think of anything to say. What was there to say?

The café door opened. A rough-looking man in a crumpled, stained shirt strode in. Pari's heart started to pound. Was that him?

The man glanced around the café. He strolled across the room and passed right by the Hakimians' table.

"Nice weather today," he said politely. He didn't stop but walked right on into the bathroom.

The Hakimians looked at each other. This was it. No goodbyes, no hugs or kisses. No nothing. It was too dangerous.

Pari and Maheen got up from the table casually.

"We're just going to the bathroom, Maman," Pari said lightly.

They walked as calmly as they could to the bathroom. No looking back; that might give the game away. They opened the door and stepped inside. And that was it. They were gone.

Chapter 1

THE CALM BEFORE THE STORM

Tehran, Iran, 1973

In a quiet neighborhood in Tehran, the door of the Hakimian family burst open. Two eight-year-old girls with jet-black hair rushed in. The first girl was pulling her sister's hand.

"Come on, Maheen! You're so slow!"

"Pari! Maheen! Where have you been?" Mrs. Hakimian asked the identical twins. "It's almost Shabbat!"

"I'm sorry, Maman," Maheen said quietly, her head down. "We forgot the time."

"Yes, Maman!" Pari took over the conversation. "We were playing at Banu's house!" Pari's big brown eyes danced. "You know we're always there!"

Banu was the twins' best friend and neighbor. But

An alleyway in Tehran

she was also an Iranian Muslim. Now that Iran was ruled by the Shah, who was tolerant toward the Jews, Muslim and Jewish children often played together.

There was a soft knock, and the door opened again.

"Baba!" the twins cried out, and threw themselves on their father.

Mr. Hakimian looked very tired, but his face lit up at the sight of his wife and daughters.

Mr. Hakimian worked hard as a truck driver. He often didn't come home until late at night. But he made a decent salary, enough to buy the family a comfortable home in a good neighborhood.

THE CALM BEFORE THE STORM • 13

The Hakimians were not wealthy like many Jews in Iran. Those Jews lived in huge mansions and owned property and stores. But the twins' family lived a comfortable life. Their four-bedroom house stood alone on its own grounds, with lemon and pomegranate trees in the garden.

"Where are Jimmy and Gallin?" Mr. Hakimian asked. "Are they home yet?"

"Yes. Jamshid is in the shower and Gallin is getting dressed," Mrs. Hakimian replied.

The twins looked at each other and giggled.

A typical street in Tehran in the 1980s, showing a mixture of older buildings and modern skyscrapers

"So we still have plenty of time then, till Gallin decides what to wear?" Pari asked.

Maman smiled. Eleven-year-old Gallin thought only of pretty dresses and hair ribbons.

"And why is Jimmy taking a shower now?" Pari complained. "It's my turn to go first! Just because he's the oldest he thinks he can do whatever he wants! Huh!"

Jimmy's real name was Jamshid but everyone except Maman always called him Jimmy. He was the eldest son, five years older than the twins.

Finally, after a lot of racing around, everyone was dressed in their Shabbat clothes. The girls had their hair neatly tied back with satin ribbons. They stood

View of Tehran with the mountains in the background

around Maman as she lit the Shabbat candles. She looked with pride and love at her four children.

"You should be blessed with a peaceful, happy life," she prayed with all her heart.

The family was joined by aunts, uncles, and cousins for the Shabbat meal.

"Pari, come help bring the *gondhi* to the table," her mother called. Pari jumped up to help. *Gondhi* was Pari's absolute favorite food. Delicious balls of ground chicken and chickpea flour, flavored with turmeric and cardamom, they were boiled in the chicken soup. Pari looked forward to it all week.

After the meal, Pari sat back and looked around. All her family was around her, and they had lots of good food. Life was great.

If she had only known what would happen in the coming years, she would not have been smiling.

Chapter 2
WINDS OF CHANGE

Tehran, Iran, June 1978, five years later

There was a frantic knocking on the door.

"Open up! Let me in!" a voice outside screamed.

Mrs. Hakimian rushed to the door and unlocked it. Jimmy fell through the entrance. His face was covered in blood.

"What happened to you?!" she cried.

"They threw stones at me!" Jimmy moaned, collapsing on the floor. He was a young man now, already eighteen, but he was crying.

"Who was it? Who did this to you?" his mother demanded, wiping blood from his face with her apron.

Jimmy's answer shocked her.

"The Nuri boys! They were my friends!" Jimmy cried out. His wounds hurt. But what hurt more was that his friends had turned on him. "We got into an argument. They started saying the Ayatollah was right and that all us Jews were spies for the Zionist state."

"So where did all this blood come from?!" his mother demanded.

"Some more boys came along and joined in. Then everyone got heated up and they all started throwing stones at me. I was lucky to get away alive!"

Mrs. Hakimian closed her eyes. For a while, things had been getting bad for the Jews of Iran. Now they had just gotten a whole lot worse. Many strict Muslims were against the secular rule of the Shah and spoke up against him. The Shah's most influential opponent was the Ayatollah Khomeini.

Official portrait of Mohammed Reza Pahlavi, Shah of Iran

The Shah had sent Khomeini into exile years ago, before the twins had been born. But in the last few years, he was becoming more powerful. For months now, there had been violent demonstrations in the streets against the Shah. People wanted the Ayatollah Khomeini to come back. Worst of all, because the Shah was friendly with America and Israel, the Muslims who were against him were now turning against their Jewish neighbors.

"What happened?" Pari cried as she and Maheen raced down the stairs.

The twins were thirteen now and in high school — a mixed school where Jews and Muslims learned together. But times had changed. Jewish and Muslim children no longer played with each other. And Banu was no longer the twins' best friend. Her parents wouldn't let her play with Jews anymore.

The twins knew the streets were no longer safe for a Jew alone. Each day, they came straight home after school and stayed there.

The family waited anxiously for Mr. Hakimian to come home from work to tell him the news. Now that he was driving a taxi instead of a truck, he often came home earlier. But tonight, of all nights, he was late.

"I'm sorry," he said when he finally arrived. His face was tired and tense. "The roads were blocked. There was another demonstration. There were hundreds of them. They were burning tires and chanting 'Death to the Shah!'"

Taxis on the streets of Tehran

Then Mr. Hakimian saw Jimmy, his face all bandaged up. After the violence he had seen, he didn't need to ask questions. He understood.

"Elias, what will be?" Mrs. Hakimian asked her husband. "What can we do?"

"You heard what Rabbi Zardazeh said in the synagogue on Shabbat?" Mr. Hakimian said.

The twins were sitting on the stairs. They were too young to join the discussion. But they couldn't help hearing... And they had heard the rabbi too. Quietly but firmly, he had told the Jews in his community that if they could leave Iran now, they should.

"I know," Mrs. Hakimian replied with a worried frown. "You know my cousin Sina has already left with his family. And my sister Dalia told me they're leaving as soon as they can."

The twins, sitting on the stairs, looked at each other in shock.

"Leave Iran?" Maheen whispered to Pari. "How could we?"

"You want to get stones thrown at you too?" Pari hissed back. "I wish we could leave right now! Shh! I want to hear what Baba says."

"Well," they heard their father answer. "I don't think it's as bad as all that. Maybe if we keep our heads down and stay out of trouble, things will calm down. And anyway, we can't leave now — we don't have the money."

And so the Hakimians, like most of the other Jews of Iran, continued on with their lives.

January 17, 1979, six months later

Mr. Hakimian had come home early. His face was drawn.

"Quick, turn on the radio!" he ordered.

Pari ran to switch it on. The family sat in silence as the announcer came on the air.

"Good evening, Iran. We have breaking news. His

Imperial Majesty, Mohammad Reza Pahlavi, Shah of Iran, has fled the country. From today, Iran has no ruler."

The Hakimian family sat in horrified silence. What was there to say? What would be now, without the Shah to protect the Jews from the fanatic Muslims?

Chapter 3

THE REVOLUTION

February 1, 1979

Mrs. Hakimian was at home, preparing supper. The twins were sitting at the kitchen table, cutting vegetables.

"Maman, will you have time to finish sewing us our new dresses before Shabbat?" Pari asked.

Their mother was just about to answer, when the door flew open. Mr. Hakimian rushed in. He was flushed and out of breath.

"I had to leave my taxi in the street and run home! All the roads are blocked! There are thousands of people everywhere, marching, chanting. It's chaos!"

Mrs. Hakimian stopped in the middle of chopping an onion. Knife still in hand, she turned to her husband.

"Another demonstration?" She sighed. Demonstrations in the street happened almost every day lately.

"No, no! This is much worse!" Mr. Hakimian said. He sat down at the kitchen table and put his head in his hands. "Much, much worse. The Ayatollah Khomeini has come back from exile! And millions of fanatic Muslims are out to welcome him back!"

Mrs. Hakimian sat down suddenly beside her husband. This was terrible news indeed. Muslims like these believed that Islam was the only true religion. If they were in control, anyone who wasn't Muslim — especially a Jew — was in danger.

Pari and Maheen were terrified. Would the wild demonstrations reach their house? What would they do if they did?

"Baba, what shall we do?" Pari asked her father fearfully.

"Nothing," Mr. Hakimian sighed. "There's nothing we can do. Just stay inside and pray."

Ayatollah Khomeini returning to Iran from exile

So the Hakimians, like the rest of the Jews of Iran, stayed in their homes and prayed. They could hear the noise from inside the house; it was terrifying. The Shah's troops were still loyal to him, and they were fighting against the Ayatollah's supporters. There was shouting and screaming every day. People burned garbage cans in the streets. And the sound of shooting could be heard everywhere. Mr. Hakimian made sure all the doors were kept locked, and no one left the house. The twins were frightened. But they were also teenagers. Stuck at home for days on end, they were getting restless.

"How much longer do we have to stay locked up like this?" Pari complained to her mother.

"I don't know, Pari dear," Mrs. Hakimian said. "As long as it takes."

Mrs. Hakimian was worried too. They had food in the house, but if the fighting went on much longer, it would run out.

In the end, it didn't take long. After ten days of fighting, the Shah's troops were overpowered. They surrendered, and the radical Muslims were now in charge.

The Hakimians — and all the Jews — soon felt the results of the new Islamic regime. The first thing to affect the twins was the new law about head coverings. Not long after the Ayatollah had been declared Supreme Ruler, Pari and Maheen came home from school one day to find Mrs. Hakimian unwrapping a package. She pulled out four shawls, in four different colors.

"What's that?" Pari asked.

"These are for us," Mrs. Hakimian said heavily. "One for me, one for you, one for Maheen, and one for Gallin. It's a hijab. From now on, we have to cover our hair with a shawl every time we go outside. It's the law. They said any woman or girl caught without their hair covered would be arrested."

"But why?!" Pari burst out. She and Maheen had beautiful black hair and she didn't want to cover it. "We're not Muslims, we're Jews! Why do we have to cover our hair like the Muslims?"

Mrs. Hakimian smiled sadly at her rebellious daughter.

"Because the Muslims rule Iran now, and we have to follow Muslim law now," she explained.

"What do you mean?" Pari demanded. "You mean

Store selling hijabs

Street protests against the Shah

we can't be Jews anymore? Can't we go to synagogue and keep Shabbat?"

"Well, the Ayatollah actually said that he would protect the Jews," Mrs. Hakimian said. "He said we would be free to practice our religion. So don't worry. Everything will be okay."

Pari could hear from Maman's voice that she wasn't really so sure everything would be okay. None of the Jews trusted the Ayatollah's promises at all. But Pari understood that her mother didn't want to worry them, so she just smiled back and said nothing.

Like all the Iranian Jews, the Hakimians prayed that things would calm down. They hoped that if they kept a low profile, nothing worse would happen to them.

Chapter 4
DIFFICULT DECISIONS

Every Shabbat when the Hakimians went to the synagogue, more people were missing.

"The Almasis are gone," Mr. Hakimian said sadly to his wife.

"And the Simnegars," she said.

"It was easy for them. They had plenty of money, and connections too," Mr. Hakimian said.

It was true. There were no laws — yet — stopping Jews from leaving Iran. But you needed plenty of money. So at first it was the wealthy Jews who were leaving. But every Jew was wondering: should I leave or not?

More and more Jews were fleeing the country. At the same time, it was getting harder to leave.

A few years later, the Islamic regime passed a new law. This law didn't let a Jewish family leave Iran together. If one member of the family left, the govern-

Iranian passport from the period of the Shah's rule

ment took away the passports of the rest of the family. Since Jewish families could no longer leave legally, they turned to illegal methods. Stories of smugglers were whispered in the synagogue. These smugglers would, for a price, take groups of Jews across the mountains to Turkey.

Soon, everybody knew the names of people with connections to the smugglers. Everyone knew where to go and what to do. The Hakimians also wanted to leave. But they didn't have enough money to pay the smugglers, so they remained at home.

1983, four years later

It was time for the twins to graduate high school. They were eighteen now, and lucky to have been able to finish school. Most of the schools where Muslims and Jews learned together had been closed down. It was also time for a family decision. Things were getting worse every day for the Iranian Jews, and there didn't seem to be much hope for the future. The Hakimians had to decide. Should they try to leave?

Could they leave? How? How could they afford it? And, most importantly, who should go?

The Hakimians met up at their family home. Their family had grown. Jimmy was now married with two children. He arrived with his wife, Leila, and their mischievous little boys. Gallin had also recently married, and came with her new husband, Samson. Everyone settled themselves around the big table, and Mrs. Hakimian brought out rice cookies and hot tea. Mr. Hakimian looked around at everyone.

"We all know things are not looking good here for the Jews," he began. "And we all know Jews who have left Iran, both legally and illegally. We need to decide what to do — stay or go. Anyone have anything to say?"

Demonstrators storm the American Embassy in Tehran

Jimmy spoke up. "Leila and I don't want to go now," he said. "I'm just getting started with my antique store. And anyway, we would never make it across the mountains with the children."

"I agree," said Gallin. "We're staying too. I'm not brave enough to climb mountains. And who knows if it will be any better where you end up?"

"Well," Mr. Hakimian replied. "You all know I can't go now because of my leg, and that means Maman stays too." Mr. Hakimian had had a bad accident driving his taxi. He'd been in the hospital for months. Now he was home, but his leg was badly damaged and it was hard for him to walk. "That leaves just you, girls. What do you say?"

"I want to go!" Pari burst out. "I've had enough. Enough of the teasing and name-calling at school. Enough of being stuck at home because it's not safe to walk in the streets alone. Enough of being afraid. I want a normal life!"

"What about you, Maheen?" Mr. Hakimian turned to Pari's quiet twin.

"I don't know," she said with a worried voice. "I hate what's happening here, but I still love Iran. It's my home. I don't want Pari to go on her own, but I'm terrified of going over the mountains."

Pari turned on her in sudden anger. "Don't you want a normal life too? Don't you want to get married? You know the boys our age are all escaping, if they haven't already. There will be no one left to marry! Do you want to stay single and miserable all your life?"

Maheen hung her head. She knew her sister was right, but she wasn't as tough as Pari. But she couldn't stay behind if her twin was going. She raised her head.

"Okay," she said, trying to sound brave. "I'll come too."

Chapter 5

SECRETIVE PREPARATIONS

Making the decision to escape from Iran was hard. But even though the twins had made the decision, they still couldn't leave yet. Taking Jews across the mountains was very dangerous, and smugglers demanded a very high price. The Hakimians didn't have enough money for that, so the twins had to earn it somehow.

"You can get work sewing," Mrs. Hakimian suggested. "I've taught you both well. You know how to make beautiful clothes!"

And indeed, both the girls had inherited Mrs. Hakimian's talent for sewing. She spread the word around the Jewish community that the twins were looking for sewing jobs. Soon, they had more than enough work on their hands. Pari concentrated on making clothes, and Maheen concentrated on embroidering sheets and tablecloths. Working from the

Iranian banknotes in use during the reign of the Shah

safety of their home, they were earning good money. But not a penny of it was spent. At the end of every week, the girls handed their earnings to their father. He deposited the money into the bank so that it was safe. That was the girls' "escape fund."

The time went by. Every week in synagogue, the Hakimians heard of yet another family whose son had disappeared, or even a young couple. Everything had to be kept secret so the authorities wouldn't find out. So when someone decided to escape, he wouldn't tell anyone, not even his neighbors and friends. He would just disappear. But everyone knew where he had gone.

The latest news was that the escape route via Turkey was not good anymore. The Jewish family that had been arranging visas had been arrested — trapping hundreds of Jews in Istanbul with no way out. So now the smugglers were taking the Jews across the mountains to Pakistan, to the city of Karachi. There, Jewish organizations were helping the refugees get visas for Israel or America.

Meanwhile, things were getting worse for the Jews in Iran. One day, Mrs. Hakimian came home in tears.

"The Muslims took my parents' house!" she wept. "They came last night. They told my father they wanted their home to use as a Muslim school. They told him if he didn't give it to them they would throw him in jail. He was terrified. He was forced to give it to them. My beautiful home that I grew up in! Now my parents have no home!"

Pari tried to comfort her mother. But there wasn't much she could say. It wasn't the first time the Islamic regime had stolen Jewish property. The Muslims knew the Jews had no choice. Many, like Mrs. Hakimian's parents, were forced to give up their homes for fear

A map showing the escape options from Tehran to Istanbul and Karachi

of their lives. And others left behind everything they owned, just to get out safely.

Summer 1987, four years later

One evening, once the supper was cleared away, Mr. Hakimian turned to the twins.

"Girls, I've checked the money in the bank account. We have enough now to pay the smugglers for both of you to escape!"

"At last!" Pari cried out. "We've been working like slaves for four years and never took a penny for ourselves! And things are even worse now. When can we leave?"

"Not so fast, Pari," Mr. Hakimian calmed his excited daughter. "First we have to take the money out of the bank account. And we can't take it out all at once; it would look too suspicious. I'll have to take it out a bit at a time. It will take a few weeks. When we have all the money safe at home, then we can get in touch with the smugglers."

Mr. Hakimian spoke again. "It will be Tishah B'Av soon. You know it's not good for Jews to travel then or during the weeks before. I will arrange with the smugglers for after Tishah B'Av so there should be a blessing on your escape."

And so it was. Slowly, one small sum at a time,

Mr. Hakimian took out the twins' hard-earned savings from the bank. It was a great deal of money, almost enough to buy an apartment. Finally, it was all safe at home, hidden under the mattress. Tishah B'Av came and went. The Iranian Jews fasted. They felt the real pain of exile living under strict Muslim rule in Iran.

Mr. Hakimian made contact with the smugglers. It wasn't hard. Everyone knew someone who knew someone who knew smugglers. The information was passed from Jew to Jew in the synagogues, often through the women. Not every smuggler was trustworthy; sometimes they took the money and never came back. And sometimes they were caught and thrown in jail or even killed. The smuggler Mr. Hakimian chose had already helped his cousins to escape, so he trusted him.

"Have the money ready at ten tonight," the smuggler ordered him abruptly over the phone. "Someone will come to collect it." He hung up, without giving his name.

The Hakimians hung around the house, waiting nervously. Ten came and went — no one. What had happened? They were getting even more nervous. What if it was a trap and the man had reported them to the police? Finally, at a quarter to eleven, there was a quick, quiet knock on the door.

"Let me in and close the door quickly," the man standing on the doorstep ordered. He entered the house and stood in the hallway. He was dark-skinned and unshaven, with dirty clothes.

"I couldn't come before. There was an army patrol in the streets, and it was too dangerous," he explained. "Now, where is the money? Half now, and I come back for the other half when we get word that they made it to Karachi."

Mr. Hakimian handed it to him silently. The man counted it. "Okay. Now listen. You need to be ready to go within two weeks. Someone will call you and give you instructions. Don't bring anything, just what you can carry in your pockets. We will give you food."

That was it. The man left as quickly and silently as he had come. Now all the girls had to do was wait for the call. They had nothing to pack, nothing to prepare. But they couldn't leave the house in case

Yusef Abad Synagogue in Tehran

the call came. The whole family was tense, waiting for the call.

"When will it be?" Pari burst out one day. "Enough already! How much longer can we wait?!"

"Pari, my dear daughter! You're so excited to leave your mother and father?" Mrs. Hakimian rebuked her gently.

"No, Maman! Of course not!" Pari flung her arms around her mother. "Of course I don't want to leave you and Baba! But we don't have a life here! You know that!"

"I know," Mrs. Hakimian said softly. She hugged Pari back. "It's okay, I understand."

But really, Pari was excited. Not to leave her family and home behind, of course. She would miss her parents, and even Iran, terribly. But she was young. She wanted a life, a normal life, free from fear.

When would the call come?

Chapter 6
TIME TO GO

The Hakimians were just sitting down to eat together. It was a simple midweek meal. Mrs. Hakimian brought a steaming bowl of rice and lentils to the table. Pari put a big bowl of green vegetables on the side, and Maheen brought a jug of water.

Suddenly, the phone rang. Everyone looked at each other nervously. Could it be the call they had been waiting for for two weeks? Mrs. Hakimian looked across the table at her husband.

"Elias, best you should answer it..."

Mr. Hakimian nodded silently and got up.

He picked up the receiver from its place on the dresser along one wall of the living room.

"Hello?"

Mr. Hakimian didn't give his name over the phone. The Jews in Iran had learned to be cautious.

They knew how to keep quiet and keep secrets, and not to tell anyone anything if they didn't have to. It was safer that way.

The person on the other end of the phone didn't identify himself either. It was safer for him that way too. "The goods need to be in Zahedan on Thursday," said a rough voice. "Café Dariush. Two o'clock. Make sure they are in blue. Someone will pick them up. He will give you the password 'Nice weather today.' You understand?"

"Yes, yes," stammered Mr. Hakimian. "I can remember all that. But wait! What should we bring? Food, clothes, anything?"

"Nothing!" was the curt reply. "We can't carry anything extra. We have everything that is needed. Remember — Zahedan, Thursday!"

The caller hung up.

Mr. Hakimian replaced the receiver with a shaking hand. He looked over at his wife. She was sitting at the table with her head in her hands.

"So this is really it," he said. He tried to smile at his wife.

She tried to smile back at him but it was a weak, teary smile. The girls, too, sat silently. Everyone had forgotten about the steaming rice and lentils. And no one had an appetite anymore.

Pari was the first one to rouse herself from the sadness that surrounded the soon-to-be-parted family.

"Look, there's no point being sad. We all agreed

Iran Air plane, similar to the plane on which the girls flew from Tehran to Zahedan

that we have to do this. Let's not spoil our last few days together."

Maheen perked up too. "Pari's right, Maman. And we have things to do. We need plane tickets to Zahedan for Thursday, and today is already Tuesday."

There wasn't much to take care of in the next two days. Buying plane tickets to Zahedan wasn't a problem. Situated at the foot of the mountains that divided Iran and Pakistan, Zahedan was a popular tourist spot. There was a big modern airport there with regular flights from Tehran. Even Jews could fly there without raising suspicions.

There was no packing to do either. The smugglers

had told them not to take anything, not even food. But the girls couldn't leave without some memento of their family. Who knew when they would see them again? So Pari and Maheen rummaged through the family photo album. They each chose a few personal favorites and tucked them deep into the pockets of the blue clothes they would be wearing. The girls were the "goods" the man on the phone had mentioned. They had to wear a certain color so the man in the café in Zahedan would be able to identify them.

Thursday came all too quickly. Before they left for the airport, Mrs. Hakimian brought out a steaming bowl of rice with eggplant and chicken for their final meal at home. The twins and their parents sat around the oval dining table, where they had eaten so many family meals together. Mrs. Hakimian was sad and silent. Who knew when she would next cook a meal for her beloved daughters? Her husband was sad too, but practical.

"So, girls, remember! Call us as soon as you can when you arrive in Karachi. We'll know you are there when the smuggler comes to get the second half of the money. But we won't be able to relax until we hear your voices and know you are really okay."

"Yes, Baba," said Maheen quietly.

Even the usually cheerful Pari was subdued. Suddenly, she threw herself into her mother's arms.

"Oh, Maman! I'm so scared! Who knows what will happen to us and if we will ever see you and Baba again!"

Mrs. Hakimian hugged Pari tightly and pulled Maheen into her arms too. Then the twins turned to their father. He hugged them tightly too, with tears in his eyes.

"We have to say goodbye now, girls; there can be no goodbyes in the café in Zahedan. But it's not goodbye forever. We will see you again, when the time is right. And always remember how much we love both of you!"

It was time to go. The girls dried their tears, and looked around them for the last time. They were trying to remember every detail of the home they had grown up in. They would probably never see it again.

A few hours later, the Hakimians were on the plane to Zahedan. Iran is a very big country. Even by plane, the journey from Tehran to Zahedan took two hours. The girls and their parents didn't speak much

The bazaar in Zahedan, on the border between Iran and Pakistan

during the flight. They were too nervous and worried about what was going to happen. And, of course, they were also scared somebody might overhear them and get suspicious.

They arrived safely in Zahedan Airport. They had no luggage, so they were free to walk straight outside. There were no security checks for the Hakimians because they had only come from Tehran. But there were plenty of armed guards patrolling the airport. Just looking at them made Pari feel nervous. She felt like it was written all over her face that she was fleeing Iran.

"Come on, Pari," Maheen pulled her sister along. "Let's get out of here."

Outside, the sun was bright and hot. It was the middle of the day in the middle of a typically hot and sticky Iranian summer.

"Where is the café?" Mrs. Hakimian asked her husband.

Maman seems to have aged so much in the last few days, Pari thought. *All this worrying and waiting has been so hard for her. And now we are leaving her and she doesn't know when she will see us again. I think it must be harder for her to stay than for us to go.*

"The café is just up this side street," said Mr. Hakimian, leading his wife and daughters up a quiet alleyway. "There, you see? Café Dariush, the one with the flowerpot by the door."

Pari and Maheen glanced at each other before they

walked in the door. *Here we go*, their glance seemed to say. *There's no turning back now.*

Mr. Hakimian chose a table in the middle of the café. He wanted to make it easy for the smuggler to be able to walk past their table without attracting attention. The café was quiet; Mr. Hakimian didn't know if that was good or bad. If it was quiet, then perhaps no one would notice their meeting. But then maybe people would notice just because it was so quiet. And Mr. Hakimian didn't much like the look of the café. It was dark and dirty, not the type of place he would usually take his wife and daughters.

"What can I get you?" asked the waiter, a sullen, bored-looking youth.

Traditional café in Iran

"Oh, er, bring us four sherbets, please," Mr. Hakimian ordered. A delicious sweet, cool sherbet drink would make them all feel better.

The sherbets the waiter brought were surprisingly good. But no one was thinking about sherbet. Everyone was thinking of just one thing: would the smuggler show up?

The time seemed to pass so, so slowly. They tried to make conversation, but no one could think of anything to say. What was there to say?

The café door opened. A rough-looking man in a crumpled, stained shirt strode in. Pari's heart started to pound. Was that him?

The man glanced around the café. He strolled across the room and passed right by the Hakimians' table.

"Nice weather today," he said politely. He didn't stop but walked right on into the bathroom.

The Hakimians looked at each other. This was it. No goodbyes, no hugs or kisses. No nothing. It was too dangerous.

Pari and Maheen got up from the table casually.

"We're just going to the bathroom, Maman," Pari said lightly.

They walked as calmly as they could to the bathroom. No looking back; that might give the game away. They opened the door to the bathrooms, and stepped inside. And that was it. They were gone.

Chapter 7
HIDING OUT

Inside the bathroom, it was hot and stuffy, with a foul aroma. But the girls were too tense to care about a bad smell. They weren't staying long anyway.

Though the twins didn't know it, there were two good reasons why smugglers used Café Dariush as the meeting place. First, it was on a small, quiet side street where few police or soldiers visited. And secondly, the bathroom was unusual in that it had two entrances — one from inside the café, and one from the alleyway at the back. That made the café the perfect place for smugglers to pick up their "goods."

Of course, the owner of the café knew just what was going on. But he kept quiet — for a price. The smugglers made sure to slip him a generous sum of money every so often to keep him happy. What they didn't know was that he would have kept quiet even without the money. The café owner was one of the thousands who hated the new Islamic regime and was happy to help people escape from it, Jews or not.

But Pari and Maheen knew nothing of all this. They were terrified someone would stop them. The man had already disappeared, so the girls followed him cautiously out of the bathroom and outside into the alley. No words passed between them. They had been warned beforehand not to talk on the way, just to follow the man who had given them the password in the café.

He was a few yards ahead of them, strolling casually with a cigarette in his hand as though he was just

A road on the Iran-Pakistan border

taking a leisurely walk. The girls tried to do the same, forcing themselves to walk slowly and calmly, though they were terrified of losing sight of him.

They had no idea where they were going or what was going to happen. All they could do was follow him and trust they would be safe. They wanted to hold hands like they used to when they were little girls walking to school together. But they were scared that even that might look suspicious; after all, they were grown women now.

The man continued down the alleyway and then, suddenly and smoothly, disappeared into a courtyard on the left. The girls followed. When they reached the courtyard, they too swiftly entered, hoping no one had noticed them.

Inside the courtyard, the man was waiting for them. He beckoned to them.

The courtyard was like many in Iran, a square, stone-paved area used by the apartments surrounding it to hang out laundry and also for the women to sit and socialize. In many neighborhoods, such courtyards had colorful flowers, lemon and pomegranate trees, even a fountain. But this was clearly not one of the better neighborhoods. The courtyard was dirty and almost bare — no flowers, no trees, and not even any fresh laundry hanging out to dry. The place looked as though no one lived there.

He led them into the apartment in the corner of the courtyard. Inside, it was dark after the bright sunshine. But when Pari's eyes began to adjust, she saw they were not alone. Around the walls of the room were benches covered in rugs, like in many traditional Iranian homes. And sitting on the benches, in groups of two or three, were a number of other people — maybe a dozen or so, Pari estimated. They all looked up fearfully as the girls came in, and one man, who looked to be in his mid-twenties, jumped up, ready to defend himself if necessary.

"Calm down!" the smuggler spat out. "It's only me. Here are a few more of you. Now wait here patiently and be quiet," he told Pari and Maheen. "I'll come back later to get you all. Remember — no one goes out of the apartment, and no noise!"

And with that, he was gone.

The girls found a corner of the room and sank down on the benches. The rugs were none too clean, but they barely noticed.

"What now?" Maheen whispered to her twin.

"I've no idea," Pari whispered back.

"Don't worry, girls," a voice spoke softly beside them.

The girls turned around. Beside them was a woman, with a man next to her who appeared to be her husband. The woman's hair was covered by the required headscarf, but in the dim light, her face looked kind.

"This is where the smugglers gather everyone together before the trip over the mountains," she explained. "Don't be afraid. No one will hurt you. The smugglers take care of their 'merchandise' very well so they'll get the rest of their money."

That made sense to the girls, and they calmed down a little.

"Try to get some rest," the kind woman advised them. "You'll need all your strength for getting across the mountains. Here, drink a little water."

The smugglers had left a few jugs of water and a pile of *lavash* — long, thin, flat Persian bread. The girls took a little bread, though they were too nervous to be hungry, and drank a bit. They tried to snuggle up in the corner to rest a little, but it was hard. The rest of

A typical rural home in Iran

the people in the room were all waiting too, and the atmosphere was tense. After a few hours, the smugglers brought in another group, two boys in their late teens.

It was dark by now, and the girls tried to get some sleep on the benches. The hours went by, slowly, slowly. Pari was half asleep when suddenly she was rudely awakened.

"Everybody up! Let's go!"

It was the man from the café. It had been early afternoon when he'd met them; now it was the middle of the night.

"Everyone, listen! We're walking to the foot of the mountains now, where we have to wait until the time is right to get past the guards. Now we have to walk through the town. It's late and there shouldn't be anyone on the streets, but I want total silence from everyone. Anyone talks, we leave them behind. Understand?"

The group all nodded. They filed out silently into the empty streets, and quickly and quietly followed the smuggler through the streets of the town. The houses grew fewer and fewer, and then they were out of the town and on a rough track heading toward the mountains. There were no streetlights here, just the light of the moon.

After what seemed like hours, the smuggler stopped. Above them, the girls could see the mountains silhouetted in the moonlight. The smuggler led the group into a crevice between the rocks, where they were hidden from sight.

A wall built on the Iran-Pakistan border to prevent smuggling

"Now, you wait here," he told them. "There are guards ahead, on this side of the mountains. When it's safe to move, we'll come get you. Wait, and remember — no noise!"

He was gone. The girls and the rest of the party seated themselves among the boulders and waited, yet again. How long would they have to wait this time?

The sun rose and set once more. There was little shade, and the escapees suffered from the baking sun during the day. After sunset, they were chilled; the mountains get cold at night even in the summer. And they were all hungry, thirsty, tired, and scared.

Then, as suddenly as he had disappeared, the smuggler suddenly reappeared, with another man.

"Okay, the guards won't give us any trouble now. It's time to go! To the mountains!"

Chapter 8
OVER THE MOUNTAINS

The mountains looked enormous from where the group was standing, right at the bottom. *How will we ever get across them?* Pari wondered. And in the dark too; she hoped the moonlight would be enough for them to see by. There was just enough light for her to see the faces of the other people in their group, and she suspected they were all thinking the same thing.

The smuggler who had arrived with the man from the café now stood in front of the group of nervous Jews. He was tall and tanned and looked tough.

"Listen to me." He spoke very quietly but firmly. "We are going on the track across the mountains now. If you do exactly as I tell you, you will be safe. If you don't, we might all get caught or even killed. Is that clear?"

Everyone murmured in agreement.

"First rule — absolute silence! No talking, and walk quietly so no one can hear us. The Iranian border guards are not far away. We waited till now, when they're eating inside their hut and aren't paying attention to what's happening outside. But if they hear talking or any other noise, we're in trouble.

"Second rule — no one goes off the path. It's narrow in places, and there are dangerous drops. I know where I'm going, just follow me and everything will be okay. We walk single file, one after the other. All clear?"

Pari and Maheen were scared, like the others, but glad to finally be on their way. So they nodded and joined the line following the tall smuggler. The man from the café brought up the rear, to keep watch from behind.

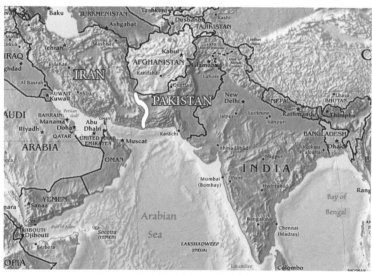

A map showing the border between Iran and Pakistan

Slowly, carefully, quietly, the line of people made their way up the narrow mountain path. Single file, their heads down, seeing only the path and the feet of the person in front of them, no one made a sound. But Pari could feel her heart beating so loudly that she thought the guards must surely hear it.

As they reached the first peak, the tall smuggler silently pointed down to the left. There, less than a hundred yards below them, was the border guards' hut. The smuggler put his fingers to his lips. Hopefully, the guards were busy eating inside and wouldn't hear or see them. But they couldn't take any chances.

They moved on, the tall smuggler leading the way, treading silently and softly. The rest of the group followed in his footsteps. Suddenly, the kind lady who had spoken to Pari slipped, and a shower of small stones tumbled down the mountainside.

"Get down, quick!" hissed the leader.

Everyone flung themselves flat on the ground.

One of the guards came out of the hut, wiping his mouth.

"Who's there?" he called, picking up his rifle from the ground.

"There's no one there, Arman!" came a voice from inside. "It's probably just a fox. Come finish your food before it gets cold!"

The guard took a quick glance around. He shrugged his shoulders and went back inside. The group of terrified Jews above let out their breath.

"One more mistake like that and we'll all be dead!" hissed the tall smuggler. "Come, quickly!"

They set off again, being extra careful not to dislodge any stones, and soon they were at a safe distance from the guards, and the mountain crevices shielded them from their sight. They were on their own now — just them, the smugglers, and the mountains.

The path seemed to go on forever. In the moonlight, the peaks of the mountains could be seen as gray shapes, and there were so many of them. Pari wondered how long they would have to walk for. They hadn't had anything to eat or drink since they left the apartment in Zahedan. How long ago was that? A day? Longer? She was beginning to lose track of time.

The sun was coming up. They were high in the mountains now, far from any guards, so it was safe to travel in the daylight. But as the sun rose, it got hotter and hotter. They hadn't brought water with them; the smugglers had told them not to. But now they were thirsty, and the smugglers didn't seem to have any water either.

Pari felt like she couldn't go on any further. She turned to see how Maheen was doing, right behind her. Maheen smiled at her weakly. They didn't dare speak, but it was clear to Pari that Maheen was also close to collapse.

Pari smiled back encouragingly at Maheen and gave her hand a squeeze. Somehow, they kept on putting one foot in front of the other. And then, just when it seemed the sun would fry them alive and they would surely die in the mountains, the leader called a halt. He led them a little off the track, to a shaded alcove, where, blessedly, there was a tiny spring. Everyone fell to their knees beside the spring and splashed their faces with water, drinking as much as they could with their bare hands. They lay or sat on the rough ground, utterly exhausted. But there was not to be much rest.

"We still have a long way to go and we must get to the other side of the mountains, to the Pakistani border, before sunrise tomorrow," the leader warned them. He was still speaking quietly, but with less care now that they were far from the guards. "We must keep going."

And so, after just a short while, the smugglers made them get back up and keep walking. They knew they had no choice, but it was so, so hard. They walked, and walked, and walked. The sun set, and they still walked. The moon came up, giving them a little light to see their path, and they still walked. Strange, inhuman calls echoed through the night. Pari looked fearfully around, expecting some wild wolf to pounce on them any minute.

How much longer could they go on? Pari felt Maheen's hand in hers, heavy and tired. She tightened her hold and pulled, dragging her twin along by sheer willpower. Surely, they must be almost there.

The desolate mountains of Balochistan, in South West Pakistan, where the girls crossed the border

They reached the next peak, and suddenly the leader stopped.

"Look down there!" He pointed ahead. Everyone looked eagerly forward. They were at the final peak; from there, the path led downward.

"See that hut down there? That's where we're heading, to rest. And see those lights further on? That's the Pakistani border. We're almost there!"

Chapter 9
INTO THE FIRING LINE

Now that the end of the path was in sight, the exhausted escapees found they still had a little energy left. The path down the mountain to the hut was wider and easier to navigate, and in no time they were there. Silently, the lead smuggler waved them into the rickety wooden structure. Inside were just a large dirty rug — that might once have been beautiful — thrown across the earthen floor, and a rough wooden chest in one corner. Everyone collapsed with relief onto the floor, except for the smugglers. They went over to the wooden chest and opened it.

"Here, take," they said, handing out the contents of the chest. "Eat, drink, rest. Soon, *inshallah*, we will cross the border."

The girls looked at what they had been given — bottles of Coke, and *nan-e-nochodchi*, the traditional

Persian cookies made from chickpeas and pistachios. It wasn't exactly a feast, but for the starved, parched travelers, it certainly felt like one. Pari and Maheen, along with everyone else, fell upon the food and drink with the appetite of people who hadn't eaten and drunk in days.

Then Pari lay back, resting against the wall. It was so good just to sit down, and not to be dreaming all the time about something to eat or drink.

"We're almost there," she said, turning to Maheen beside her. "The hard part is over."

"Yes, I thought I was going to collapse on the way," Maheen said with a tired smile. "But now, all we have to do is cross the border and we'll be in Pakistan, safe from the evil Iranian Islamic regime!"

One of the smugglers sitting close by overheard the girls talking and burst out laughing.

"Hah! You think the hard part is over, huh?

Pakistani ranger guarding the Pakistani border

Don't fool yourselves! Crossing the mountains might be hard, but there are no guards with rifles up there. The hardest part of the journey is now, crossing the border. The Pakistani border guards are more alert than the Iranian ones, and we still have to get past them safely."

"So what's the plan?" demanded the slim youth who had jumped up to defend himself in the apartment in Zahedan. He was young and aggressive and ready to challenge these smugglers whom he didn't really trust.

"Take it easy, boy." The taller of the smugglers looked the youth up and down. "We know what we're doing. You think you're the first group of Jews we've taken over the border? We've taken hundreds, and every time we have reached the other side safely.

"Here's what we do," the smuggler went on. "This hut is used by shepherds to sleep in when they are pasturing their flock in this area. There's a rough road from here that goes through the border, past the guards' hut. We paid one of the shepherds to bring his truck here. We're going to get you across the border in the truck."

"But how?" the persistent Jewish youth wanted to know. "They'll see there are people in the truck instead of sheep, and stop us!"

"Don't worry," the smuggler calmed everyone down. They had all heard the plan, and it didn't sound so safe. "The shepherd will be driving the truck. All the guards know him. They won't check the back of the truck. They'll just wave him through."

Pari and Maheen looked at each other. The plan sounded very dangerous, but there was nothing they could do. They were entirely in the hands of the smugglers.

"Here, put these on," the smugglers said, pulling more items from the chest. They handed out clothes to everyone. Maheen turned up her nose when she was handed a bundle.

"They don't smell too clean," she whispered to Pari.

The smuggler heard her. He laughed harshly.

Pakistani shepherds with their flocks

"Listen, princess, once we make it past the guards, we're in Pakistan. And you don't want to look like Iranian Jews, but like Pakistanis. Unless you want to get caught, of course?"

He gave Maheen a sarcastic smile, and she hastily bowed her head.

Everyone put on the clothes. For the men, there were simple linen trousers and long tunics that reached almost to the knee. For the women, there were robes in plain dark colors, with a veil that covered most of the face, even more than the Iranian hijabs.

"Until we reach Karachi, you stay in these clothes, understand?" the smugglers ordered. "And from the minute we go outside the hut until we get to Karachi, no one opens their mouth. We don't want anyone getting suspicious because you're speaking Persian, got it?"

Everyone nodded silently. And suddenly, in the silence, they heard a noise outside. It sounded like a vehicle was coming. Immediately, one of the smugglers raced to the entrance and peered out.

"It's okay. It's our man," he reported. "Let's go! Everyone — out the door and around to the back of the hut!"

The frightened Jews did as they were told. A dirty old pickup truck pulled up, with an open back. It looked — and smelled — like it was used for transporting sheep. A dark-skinned man with a turban on his head stuck his head out of the window. He spoke

Typical shepherds' hut in Pakistani mountains

to the smugglers in a language the Jews didn't understand.

"Everyone, in the back of the truck!" the lead smuggler hissed. "Lie flat on the floor, head to foot, so there will be room!"

There really wasn't room for eighteen people to lie down in the bed of the truck, even head to foot. But, somehow, they managed. The smugglers climbed in too.

"Remember! No one moves a muscle when we pass the border, and don't make a sound!"

No one would; everyone was far too scared to move or even speak.

The Pakistani shepherd revved up the engine. The truck slowly made its way along the rough dirt track that passed by the border. As they got close to the guards' hut, the truck slowed almost to a stop.

One of the guards stuck his head out of the door of the hut. The shepherd waved to him from the truck, and called out something. The guard laughed, and waved him on. The truck set off again, and Pari began to breathe again. They had crossed the border!

Suddenly, she heard shouts. Then, a terrifying sound — gunshots. The guards were firing at them!

Chapter 10
NOT SAFE YET

From the floor of the truck, Pari and the others couldn't see what was happening. But they could hear the shooting, very close to them. They were all in shock. They'd thought they'd made it over the border. But now they were going to die, just when they thought they were safe. They froze, trying to make themselves invisible.

"Don't even breathe!" the smugglers whispered.

The truck suddenly stopped. Just as suddenly, the shooting stopped too. The shepherd got out and closed his door. Casually, he strolled back to the guards' hut. He didn't seem nervous or scared. In fact, as he approached the guards he said something to them and laughed. The guards laughed too, but also pointed at him with their rifles. The shepherd got the message. He dug deep into his pocket and pulled out a roll of bills. He handed the bills to the guards, smiling. The guards gave the shepherd a friendly slap on the back. The shepherd walked away from the hut and back to his truck. The engine started, and they set off again — all without a word from the shepherd. This time there was no shooting. Pari and the others, on the floor in the back, didn't understand what was going on. But they were too terrified to ask.

As soon as they were far enough from the border, the truck stopped again. The shepherd got out again, and this time the smugglers jumped out too. They started a loud argument with the shepherd. The escapees didn't understand the local language, Balochi, but some words were similar to Persian. Finally, the smugglers came around to the back of the truck.

"Everyone out!"

There seemed to be nowhere to go — they were in the middle of an empty, dusty road. But everyone climbed out cautiously; they didn't know if someone was going to start shooting again. As soon as everyone was out, the shepherd got back into his truck. He slammed the door, and drove off in a haze of dust. The tired group of refugees huddled together on the roadside. They didn't know what would happen to them now.

"Filthy, cheating thief!" the tall smuggler growled. "He nearly got us all killed!"

"What happened back there?" the tall, slim youth plucked up the courage to ask.

"What happened? That guy cheated us, that's

what happened!" the smugglers spat out. "We paid him good money to get us over the border. He's supposed to give some of the money to the guards to keep them quiet. But he tried to be smart. He thought he could get away with keeping all the money for himself without paying off the guards. That nearly got us all killed!"

"So what now?" demanded the Jewish youth. "We're in the middle of nowhere!"

"Now? We wait for a man to come. He has a van, he will drive us to Karachi," the tall smuggler explained.

"Karachi?!" all the refugees exclaimed. "You were supposed to take us to Quetta first!"

The main street of Quetta, where most of the Iranian Jewish refugees were taken before traveling to Karachi

Quetta was the largest city in northern Pakistan. Even though it was a long way from the Iranian border, many Jewish refugees headed there before traveling to Karachi. This was for one important reason — Quetta had a branch of the UNHCR (United Nations High Commissioner for Refugees), known as the United Nations Refugee Agency. There, Jewish refugees from Iran were given refugee status. That meant they received official papers that would protect them if stopped by the Pakistani police.

Without those papers, the refugees could be stopped and arrested at any moment. And often they were. All the Jews in the group had heard stories of Jews caught in Pakistan without papers and put in jail. And so the smugglers' plan to take them directly to Karachi was very risky.

The smugglers made excuses. "Quetta is too far. It takes too long, and costs too much. You'll be okay. You'll all stay quiet in the van and go to sleep. If the police stop us, you all act asleep and we deal with them. Got it?"

The escapees got it. They didn't like it, but they had no choice. They were at the mercy of the smugglers.

A few hours later, the van finally showed up. Everyone stood up from where they'd been sitting on the side of the road. They were so tired they could barely stand. Pari was looking forward to sleeping in the van.

Somehow, everyone squeezed in. The van was not

A Pakistani banknote

designed to hold eighteen refugees, two smugglers, and a driver. The girls squashed close together, with the kind woman with the gentle voice almost sitting on top of them.

The journey was long. From the border crossing in northeast Pakistan, the drive to Karachi is close to fourteen hours. The roads were badly paved, full of potholes and bumps. And in the old minivan, which had little padding on the seats, the passengers felt every bump. There was no air conditioning, and the crowded van was soon uncomfortably hot and stuffy. Everyone was hungry and thirsty and there was still nothing to eat or drink. But despite all the discomforts, soon all the escapees fell asleep. They were so exhausted from the past few days that they were past caring.

Pari vaguely noticed the van stopping sometimes, and hearing voices. These were the checkpoints

Typical Pakistani van traveling along a desert road in Pakistan

the Pakistani police set up on every road to catch criminals, runaways, and political rebels. At each checkpoint, the Pakistani driver would casually shake hands with the policeman on duty. But hidden in his hand would be a few bills — enough to make the policeman smile and wave the van on without a check. That was how it worked in Pakistan; everyone could be paid off if you had enough money.

    Pari woke when the sun was starting to come up. In the pale light of dawn, she noticed that the view outside had changed. For hours and hours, there had been nothing outside but road and desert. Now, there were buildings, streets, stores, and even a few people already up and about.

    "Wake up!" the smugglers whispered. "We're in Karachi!"

Chapter 11
REFUGEES IN KARACHI

K*arachi*, thought Pari as she peered out of the van, *is not so very different from Tehran.* Big city, lots of big streets with big buildings. And Pari was right in some ways. Like Tehran, Karachi had once been the capital city. And like Tehran — at least since the Revolution — Karachi was a dangerous place to be. Almost ten million people lived in Karachi, of many different races and religions. There were Hindus, Muslims, Sindhis, Punjabis, and Pashtun refugees from the war in nearby Afghanistan. Violent crime was common. Weapons were everywhere.

But Pari and her sister knew nothing of all this. All they knew was what they could see from the van. At first they passed through the suburbs of the city, where the British colonial government had once lived. Here, the streets were wide and lined with trees, and the homes large and luxurious. But gradually, as they drove into the center of the city, the view changed. The streets grew narrower, dirtier, and more crowded. Even early in the morning, the streets were full of rickshaws, the three-wheeled vehicles used as taxis. The buildings here looked much older, with peeling paint and broken windows. And in many doorways, the girls saw what they thought were piles of rags... until one of the piles of rags moved, and they realized these were people sleeping on the streets. Karachi's streets were full of homeless beggars, many of them crippled and sick.

In what seemed the worst neighborhood yet, the smugglers told the driver to stop. Here were cheap motels, their broken neon signs weakly flashing on and off.

Streets of Karachi

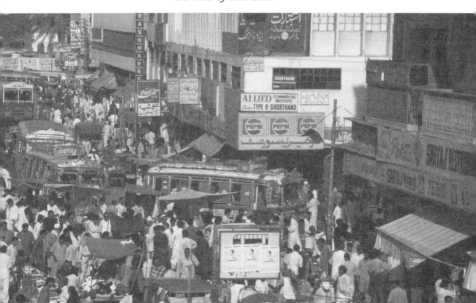

"This is where all the Jews stay." The tall smuggler turned to them. "You will be okay now. Here, we give you some money for food."

He pulled out a wad of Pakistani bills, handing them out to everyone. It wasn't very much, but it would at least help to buy some food. The girls had brought very little money with them.

Everyone got out of the van and stood on the sidewalk. They had no suitcases to take into the motel; they had nothing. The smugglers drove off quickly, and that was it. The Jews hadn't really trusted the smugglers, but they felt strangely alone without them. They were on their own in a strange, dangerous city.

Pakistani street food vendor

Inside the motel, Pari and Maheen felt better right away. In the lobby, a group of men, who were clearly Jewish, chatted in Persian. They stopped talking when they saw the refugees enter.

"Welcome, welcome!" they greeted them. "Don't worry about anything, we'll sort it all out for you. First, you all need to get some sleep. Let's get you some rooms; you can take showers and rest, and then we can talk."

"But who will pay for the rooms?" asked the youth. "None of us has enough money."

One of the men seemed to be in charge.

"Don't worry, the Jewish Agency in Israel is paying the bill for all the Iranian Jews. Relax!"

He went over to the motel clerk and spoke a few brief sentences. The clerk pushed five room keys over to him.

"Okay, here we go. They're almost full. Five rooms is all they can give you, you'll have to share."

The refugees looked at each other. Eighteen people in five rooms meant three or four to a room. And who would share with whom?

The husband of the woman with the kind voice suddenly took charge.

"Edna, you go with the two girls; they need someone older with them," he said to his wife. It was the first time they had heard her name. Now, among Jews, they felt safe enough to use their names. "And you go with them too," he said, looking at another older woman.

He went on dividing up the refugees into groups for each room. When he was done, he smiled at them all.

"Okay, everyone. I suggest we all go take showers. Let's sleep, and we'll make plans later."

The girls tramped up the narrow steps to their room and opened the door. Inside were two small beds. The thin, old mattresses were covered in crumpled, dirty sheets. There was also a scratched wooden chair and a small chest of drawers.

Pari and Maheen looked at each other in disgust, but before they could say anything, Edna spoke.

"Let's find the shower, girls," she suggested, trying to sound cheerful.

Eventually they found it, at the end of the corridor. There was only one shower for everyone on the floor. By the time the girls finally got their turn, it was late. And they soon discovered it was hardly worth waiting for; the water was cold.

But a shower was a shower. After four days of traveling, it at least washed off the grime. They were glad to take off the strange Pakistani clothes. But with no clean clothes, they had no choice but to put their own dirty, sweaty clothes back on. Everyone was exhausted and lay down to rest. It wasn't the most comfortable sleep they had ever had — two to a bed, on a thin mattress covered with dirty sheets. But they were so tired that they slept and slept, until they were woken by knocking on the door.

A group of Iranian refugees in the waiting lounge of Karachi airport

"Edna, it's me, Nissim! Open the door!"

The four women quickly got up, and Edna opened the door for her husband. He came in and sat down on the rickety chair.

"Time to make plans," he said with authority. "We need to sort out our papers so we can get out of Karachi and to Israel or America."

Pari spoke up shyly. "We were told to go to Mrs. Rachamim. Everyone said she would sort everything out."

Mrs. Rachamim was a legend among the Iranian Jewish refugees. An Afghani Jew, for years she had been the address for the tired, bewildered Jews arriving in Karachi. She somehow got papers for refugees to get out of the country. Real or not, the papers worked. She had helped hundreds of Jews on their way to Israel or America. Everyone escaping Iran was told to go to Mrs. Rachamim's house when they arrived in Karachi.

"Yes, that's what we were told too," replied Nissim. "But I have some bad news for you. Mrs. Rachamim was arrested a few months ago, and no one knows where she is."

Chapter 12
BOUND BY BUREAUCRACY

There was shocked silence in the room. Pari felt herself beginning to panic. Were they to be trapped in this dangerous, dirty city now, after all they had been through?

"Calm down," Nissim urged the girls. "We have another plan, listen! The men here told me about a Dutch Jew. He's getting papers for refugees through the Dutch government. We'll have to fly first to Amsterdam. Then we can go to the U.S. or Israel, wherever we want. Shall we try it?"

The girls, of course, agreed. It was the only plan anyone had anyway, so there was nothing to lose by trying. Nissim collected everyone's passports. He then asked everyone where they had decided to go — Israel or America. The girls had already made their decision earlier.

"I'm going to Israel, the land of the Jewish people,

and that's that!" Pari had told Maheen firmly.

Maheen had thought about maybe trying America. But, being gentle Maheen, she quietly gave in to her more forceful twin.

Nissim set off to find out about the Dutch Jew. He took Mussa with him, the husband of Lili, the second woman sharing the twins' room. Other Iranian Jewish refugees who had been in Karachi for a while had warned the new arrivals not to walk the streets alone.

The men found the Dutch Jew, a Mr. Uri Cohen. He was an elderly Orthodox Jew who had fought against the Nazis in the Dutch Underground during the Holocaust. When he found out that hundreds of

A poor neighborhood in Karachi

Iranian Jews were trapped in Karachi, Cohen decided to help. He had friends in high places, thanks to his wartime activities. He set up a system giving transit papers from the Dutch government to the refugees. They couldn't enter Holland with these papers. But they were allowed to stop there along the way to their final destination.

Cohen was staying at the Holiday Inn. Compared to the cheap motel, it was a palace. Nissim and Mussa were sent up to Cohen's room, where they were warmly welcomed. There was another man with Cohen, who was introduced as his partner, Jaap Sanders. Sanders was also an Orthodox Dutch Jew, but younger than Cohen. They had set up the system together. Now they were staying in Karachi to take care of the refugees' papers. The Dutch Jews spoke no Persian and the Persian Jews spoke no Dutch. However, the little English that Nissim and Mussa spoke helped them understand each other.

Nissim stared at Cohen and Sanders suspiciously. The Iranian Jews weren't sure whether to trust these Dutch Jews. True, other refugees had recommended them. But years of living under the Islamic regime in Iran had taught them not to trust anyone. And why were these people helping them anyway? What was in it for them? All these questions went through Nissim's mind as he shook hands with Cohen and Sanders. But he realized there wasn't really much choice. It was their only way out of Pakistan. So Nissim smiled politely and handed over the papers he'd brought — photos, their names, and dates of birth.

"Now you have to wait," Sanders told them. "We'll arrange the documents for you. But it takes time. You also need exit visas from the Pakistanis, and they do everything slowly. Come back next week to see what's happening."

Back at the motel, Nissim and Mussa shared the news with the others. Now, all they had to do was wait. But there wasn't much to do in Karachi to pass the time. Even the police had warned them not to wander the streets alone. And anyway, they had very little money.

But sometimes they simply had to go out. More than anything, everyone was anxious to call their families in Tehran. Their families knew they had arrived safely in Karachi, because the smugglers had come to collect the second half of the money. But the refugees wanted to hear the voices of their loved ones.

There was a public phone booth on the same street as the motel. Pari and Maheen, together with Edna and Mussa's wife, went out to the phone booth together. The booth was dirty and smelled terrible, but all they cared about was that the phone worked.

The girls went into the booth first. Pari dialed her parents' number in Tehran with shaking hands, Maheen beside her. They heard the phone ringing, ringing. "Pick it up, Maman, pick it up, please!" Pari begged.

The market in Karachi

They heard a voice on the other end of the line. "Hello?" Then there was a beeping.

Pari frantically pushed a coin into the slot, and the connection was made.

"Maman!" she cried, almost in tears with excitement. "We're here! We made it!"

Her mother's beloved voice came over the line. "Pari *joon*! Maheen *joon*! Are you all right? Are you eating there? Who are you with? Are you safe?"

Their mother's love and concern flowed over the phone line to the twins.

"We're okay, Maman," Pari tried to reassure her. "Please don't worry. We're safe."

"God bless you, my loves!" their mother cried. "We miss you so much! Please, take care of yourselves!"

The phone began to beep again and the girls had no more coins to insert.

"Bye, Maman! We love you! We'll call you when we get to Israel!"

The phone went dead. But their mother's loving voice stayed with the twins for a long time.

Sometimes they had no choice but to go out to buy things — like food and clothes. Pari and Maheen, like the other refugees, had only the clothes they were wearing. They had to go to the market to buy some clothes. They thought they would be safe enough together with Edna and Nissim, and Mussa and Lili.

Pari and Maheen clung to each other in fear. The streets were a mass of buses, pushcarts, people walking, bicycles, and rickshaws. In the bazaar, there were even more people, if that was possible. Everything was for sale, and the girls could barely hear themselves speak. Beggars lay on every corner and called out for money. And young, filthy boys swarmed around, ready to pick people's pockets at the first chance. The refugees quickly chose the cheapest clothes they found and left the bazaar as fast as they could.

After that, the twins stayed in their motel room as much as possible. They ate like the rest of the Jewish refugees — simple, cheap food, mostly the local *paan*, and cheese. Like most of the Iranian Jews, the twins came from a traditional, kosher home. They did their best to keep kosher during their journey. But there was no official kosher food in Karachi, so they ate only simple foods like bread, vegetables, and soft cheese.

Jaap Sanders (center, with beard) escorting a group of Iranian refugees to the departure gate at Schiphol Airport

The week was up, but Cohen and Sanders had no news. The papers weren't ready yet. Another week went by, and another. Every week on Friday, Nissim and Mussa went to the Holiday Inn to check. Every week the answer was the same — still no papers.

The Jewish holidays arrived, but the refugees had nowhere to celebrate them. No one knew where the Rachamims were. In prison — or worse? There was no shofar to blow on Rosh Hashanah, no sukkah to build for Sukkot. But fasting on Yom Kippur was something they all could do. All the refugees fasted, praying in their motel rooms without prayer books. They prayed with all their hearts that they would be saved from the trap they were in.

The holidays came to an end, and there was still

no sign of the visas. Pari and Maheen, like all the other refugees, were bored, tense, and afraid. Also, like most of the other refugees, they were running out of money. They were beginning to wonder if the Dutch Jews were really to be trusted. Maybe it was a trick by the Iranian government to catch them? Or maybe they really did want to help but couldn't get the visas? No one knew what to believe.

They had been in Karachi for more than a month. Would they ever get out of this dangerous, dirty city?

Chapter 13
EN ROUTE

Pari and Maheen were in their motel room, as usual. Chatting with Edna and Lili, they were bored and tense. Suddenly, there was loud knocking on the door.

"Let us in! It's us!" Nissim called.

The girls opened the door and Nissim and Mussa rushed in.

"They're ready! The papers! We're leaving on Monday!"

They had just come back from the Holiday Inn. The Dutch Jews had given them the good news. No one really understood why the papers had taken so long. But Cohen and Sanders had explained it to Nissim and Mussa. Now they understood what a long, complicated process it was.

First the papers were sent to the Dutch consul. He made temporary passports. Then papers of refugees going to the United States went to the Austrian embassy. An organization called Rav Tov, run by Satmar chassidim, arranged papers and flights to the U.S.

The Austrians gave visas quickly. The passports then needed exit visas from the Pakistanis. But Pakistan is a country with no sense of time. Every day is a different festival for a different religion. That means every day has a different reason not to work. Cohen and Sanders wanted to speed things up. But they knew that trying to hurry the Pakistanis would only make them slower.

But now, Cohen and Sanders had received a call from the Dutch consul. The passports were finally ready.

"So tell us all the details!" Edna nudged her husband.

"They've booked a flight to Amsterdam," he explained. "Lots of Iranian Jews will be on it, not just our group. It's for those going to the States and those going to Israel too. The airline even ordered kosher food for us all!"

Everyone was in a state of excitement. No one needed to pack. Pari and Maheen simply bought a cheap bag to hold the few clothes they'd bought in Karachi.

Monday came, and the motel was full of activity. Over half the motel's guests were leaving on the same flight. Outside was a crowd of taxis. The Iranian Jews excitedly pushed to get into them.

Cohen and Sanders were waiting at the airport. They were with an important-looking blond man.

"This is the Dutch consul," they said.

The consul handed out the precious documents to the nervous refugees. He stood next to them as the Pakistani officials checked them. Everyone held their breath, but everything went smoothly. A few short hours later, everyone was on the plane. Cohen and Sanders were there as well. As the plane took off, all the refugees breathed a deep sigh of relief. They were out of Karachi at last!

It was a long flight from Karachi to Amsterdam — eleven hours. Pari and Maheen ate hot kosher food for the first time in months. Then they fell asleep.

Karachi International Airport

In Amsterdam's Schiphol Airport, a group of people were waiting for them. With them was a tall Persian man.

"I escaped from Iran like you," he told them. "Now I live in Holland. I've come to translate for these people. They're social workers from a Jewish welfare organization, and they're here to help you."

"You have fifteen hours until your flight to Israel," Cohen and Sanders explained. "For those flying to Vienna and then the U.S., your flight is in ten hours."

With only transit visas, the refugees couldn't leave the airport. But the Dutch helpers had special permits to enter the lounge. For those who wanted, there were kosher sandwiches. Others decided to go to the airport restaurant, where they could order whatever they wanted.

"Let's go," Pari persuaded Maheen, looking forward to hot food.

Schiphol Airport is enormous and it was a long walk to the restaurant. On the way, the girls gazed at all the luxurious shops with their glittering lights and expensive goods. After the dirt and dust of Karachi, they felt like they were in a dream.

They got to the restaurant, with tempting aromas coming from it. Then Maheed sighed. "Pari, it's not kosher! We can't eat it!"

But the girls were hungry, and in the end, they decided they could eat just the bread and the French fries — and of course the ketchup. Then they were

Schiphol Airport, Amsterdam

taken to a part of the transit lounge where they could rest. Everyone appreciated the large, clean bathrooms — and enjoyed the precious hot water.

The girls had meant to sleep, but suddenly everyone wanted to talk. After being suspicious and afraid for so long, they felt safe for the first time in months. They chatted, trading names and experiences.

Then came the call for the flight to Vienna. It was time for their group to be separated. Edna and Nissim and Mussa and Lili had decided to try their luck in America.

The twins had grown very close to the two older women. It was hard to part from them. There were plenty of hugs and tears.

Finally, the call came for the El Al flight to Tel Aviv. The refugees parted from Cohen and Sanders with many thanks.

They boarded the plane with beating hearts. The plane was a special flight, full of Iranian Jewish refugees. As it took off, Pari and Maheen could hardly contain their excitement. After everything they'd been through, they were really on their way to Israel.

Chapter 14
LIFE IN ISRAEL

The captain's voice came over the loudspeaker. "Please fasten your seat belts. We are now beginning our descent into Tel Aviv."

Everyone had been sitting quietly in their seats, resting. But suddenly, everyone woke up. A wave of excitement washed over the passengers. Tel Aviv! Israel! They were almost there! Everyone was talking, shouting, gathering up their things. Pari could hardly stay in her seat. She could see the other passengers felt the same way.

Some passengers had been to Israel before. Some actually lived there. But every Jew gets excited when he approaches Israel. It doesn't matter how many times he's been there. For the Iranian refugees, however, it was the dream ending to a nightmare. They were finally safe in the Jewish people's homeland.

El Al Boeing 747 airplane

As the plane touched down, cheering and clapping filled the plane.

"Welcome to Israel!" the captain greeted everyone.

The refugees left the plane in disbelieving joy. After a brief security check, they found themselves stepping out into the arrivals lounge.

Cries and screams broke out. Iranian Jews usually have enormous families. There are lots of siblings, aunts and uncles, and cousins. And it seemed like the entire family of every Persian Jew in Israel was here to welcome these refugees. There was hugging and kissing, weeping and laughing.

Pari and Maheen felt a little lost. They had no large family in Israel. There was just an uncle they had never met, their father's brother. He had moved to Israel long before the Revolution. But they called him from Karachi to tell him when they were arriving. The problem was that they didn't know what he looked like. They were easier to recognize — after all, how many pairs of identical twin girls were on the plane?

And then their Uncle Solly spotted them and came running over. He was so like their father, just a little older.

"Welcome to Israel, Pari *joon* and Maheen *joon!*" he greeted the girls. His voice was so like their father's, it almost made them cry. They were so glad to be in Israel and have someone take care of them. But mostly, they were just so, so tired.

"Let's go home and meet your Aunt Gilda," Uncle Solly said. He picked up the small, cheap bag bought in Karachi.

Uncle Solly's house in Jerusalem was warm and welcoming. It smelled of Persian cooking and of home. His wife, Gilda, was warm and welcoming too. From there, the girls made a phone call to Iran, to their anxious parents.

The girls had made that one short call from Karachi to let their parents know they were safe. And phone calls from Israel to Iran were very expensive. Still, this was a special occasion. They had to let their parents know they were safe in Israel.

The Hakimians were overjoyed to hear from their beloved daughters. But Pari heard a note of something besides joy in their voices.

"Maman, did something happen?" she asked. "You sound strange."

"Oh, Pari!" her mother burst out crying. "You don't know how blessed you are to be in Israel and alive! We just heard about a group of Jews from Iran. They escaped over the mountains the same way you went. Twelve young boys, just fourteen or fifteen. Those guards who shot at you? They thought these poor boys were *mujahedeen*, rebels against Pakistan. They shot them all! Oh, Pari, how did we let you go alone! It could have been you!" And Mrs. Hakimian broke down in a flood of tears.

Pari and Maheen were stunned. They'd had a miraculous escape. They realized that the One Above

"Welcome to Israel" sign at Ben Gurion Airport, Tel Aviv

had guarded them all the way to Israel. Now that they were safe, they felt so grateful — and sorry for those who hadn't made it.

Solly's house was comfortable but small. And the Jewish Agency wanted the girls to go to ulpan and learn Hebrew. This way they could succeed in Israel. The girls knew how to write a little Hebrew, but couldn't speak it.

So the twins moved into a special center for immigrants, in Jerusalem. There, they learned Hebrew every day. They met lots of other Jews newly arrived in Israel. Many had also escaped from Iran, and Pari and Maheen exchanged stories and made new friends.

After the ulpan finished, the Jewish Agency paid for job training courses. Maheen decided to improve her sewing skills and work as a seamstress, as in Iran. Pari wanted to do something different. After four years of sewing to save money for their escape, she never wanted to see a needle and thread again. She took a course to become a dental assistant.

Almost a year and a half had passed since the girls' arrival. One day, Uncle Solly called Pari with a surprise suggestion.

"I have a boy for you," he said. "He would make a good husband."

Among the Jews back in Iran, marriages were

usually between distant cousins. That was why many Persian Jews looked so similar. But in Israel, they could choose Jews from other countries — and often did. Marriages between Persians and Moroccans became very popular. The boy Uncle Solly was suggesting was Moroccan.

They met, and liked each other. Shortly afterward, they were married. Pari missed her parents terribly at the wedding, but they couldn't leave Iran. But Pari was happy to find a good husband. She knew that if she had stayed in Iran, there would have been no one left to marry. By twelfth grade, the boys had all escaped. Happily married and with a new job, Pari settled down to life in Israel.

Panoramic view of Jerusalem

EPILOGUE

Pari and Maheen's incredible escape happened in 1987. That's over thirty years ago. Today, Pari is a wife, mother, and grandmother. Pari still works as a dental assistant. Her husband is an accountant. They have three children. Pari's eldest son, also an accountant, is married with children. Pari's other two children are in college.

Her twin sister Maheen is also married. She lives in Jerusalem with her family. The two are still very close.

What happened to the rest of the Hakimian family? The twins left behind their parents, their older brother Jimmy and his wife, and their sister Gallin and her husband. Mr. Hakimian, still injured, couldn't escape over the mountains. But over the years, Iran relaxed the rules a little. Jews can now leave Iran — but not to Israel. And any Jew with an Israeli stamp in their passport can't come back. That is still the law. It's almost impossible for Persian Jews in Israel to visit family in Iran.

Seven years after the twins escaped, their parents joined them in Israel. Mr. and Mrs. Hakimian were careful about their move. They sold their house. Then they told their Muslim neighbors they were moving to another neighborhood. They packed up all their things and flew to Turkey. From Turkey they flew to Israel. Gallin left Iran at the same time.

The Hakimians were just one of the many Jewish families that left Iran in the twentieth century. In 1948, there were almost a hundred fifty thousand Jews in Iran. After the State of Israel was created, many Jews left Iran for Israel. By the 1970s, just before the Revolution, about eighty thousand Jews still lived in

A baker baking "barbari" bread in Iran

EPILOGUE • 105

Traditional Persian rug

Iran. When the Islamic fanatics took control, most of the Jews left — legally or illegally.

But some stayed behind. For example, Jimmy, the twins' older brother. He was already married with small children. He also had a good business running an antique shop. He didn't want to start again with nothing in a new country. That's why many Jews stayed in Iran, even though it was dangerous. Most Jews in Iran were wealthy. Leaving Iran meant leaving their wealth behind. Life in Iran was risky, but it was familiar — the language, the neighborhood, the food.

That's why about twenty-five thousand Jews still live in Iran. That's the second-largest Jewish population in the Middle East (Israel is the first). But only about nine thousand are registered as Jews. They are afraid. Do they need to be? Surprisingly,

Jews are protected under the Iranian Constitution. They even have an official representative in the Iranian government. They're allowed to pray in their synagogues. They're allowed to practice their religion. So why are they afraid? Well, the Islamic government hates Israel. Today, Iran is threatening war against Israel. And so it's very dangerous for Jews in Iran to show any support for Israel. If they do, they are seen as enemies. That would put them in danger of being arrested as spies. In fact, thirteen Jews were arrested for that crime in 1997.

The Jews in Iran have learned how to live there. They keep their heads down, keep quiet, and keep out of trouble. The women must wear the Muslim hijab. If there are demonstrations against Israel, Jews have to demonstrate too. They need to prove their loyalty to Iran. But most Jews there feel it's worth it. Persian Jews loved their country before the Islamic fanatics destroyed it. Many Persian Jews still miss Iran very much, but can never return.

"It is the land of my birth," says Pari. "There was no place like Iran when I was a child — it was so beautiful. Without the Revolution, no Jew would have left Iran. But now everything has changed. I can never go back there."

Pari is one of the very few Persian Jews willing to tell her story. So many are afraid, even now, to speak out. When they lived in Iran they learned to stay silent to stay safe. It's now forty years after the Revolution.

But, whether they're in Beverly Hills or in Jerusalem, most Persian Jews still guard their secret stories.

Pari is unusual. She tells her story to her children and grandchildren. She tells her story to anyone who asks. Which is wonderful — without Pari there wouldn't have been this book.

How does she feel today, looking back on her life? Is it difficult to remember all the details of her scary escape? Pari is very practical.

"Yes, it's hard. But I had to make a decision back then — to stay or to run. I decided to run. It was very difficult and very dangerous. But it had a happy ending!"

An aerial view of Tehran

AUTHOR'S NOTE

I wrote this book with much *hashgachah pratis*. First, Hashem found me a Persian Jew for my husband. That made me interested in anything Persian. I was especially interested in how Persian Jews survived the 1979 Islamic Revolution.

Then I heard about Jaap Sanders. Sanders, a Dutch Jew, helped rescue thousands of Persian Jews. These Jews escaped Iran over the mountains to Pakistan. In Pakistan, Sanders helped them get to Israel or the United States. I wrote about these Jews' escape for *Mishpacha* magazine a few years ago. It was a story that hadn't been told before in English.

Many Persian Jews don't talk about their escape from Iran. They are still too scared. But Mr. Sanders introduced me to Pari. She is a Jew who escaped Iran over the mountains. She lived close to Jerusalem. And she was willing to talk to me.

Then Esther Heller of Menucha Publishers called. She wanted me to write an "escape from Iran" book, based on a true story. She didn't know I already had everything I needed to write this book!

Speaking to "Pari" (we changed her name to protect her) was thrilling. Each week she described the next stage in her and her twin sister's nerve-racking tale. She told the story in her vivid, emotional, Persian-accented Hebrew. And as she spoke, I was drawn in. I felt her tension while she was trapped in Iran waiting to get out. I felt her fear during the trek over the mountains in the middle of the night. I heard the terror in her voice as she described being shot at by border guards.

Today, most of us live comfortable lives. We are safe in our homes with our families. We can live openly as Jews without fear. Pari's story reminded me of those Jews who suffered, over the centuries, just for being Jews. Sometimes their physical lives were in danger. But more often, their identity as Jews was in danger. And so these Jews left their homes. They left their country. They left everything familiar. They left to save their spiritual lives. These brave Jews gave up everything. They did this so they could live as Jews. Most made it to safety. Some, sadly, didn't. This book is for all of them.

Shira Yehudit Djalilmand
Tzfat, Israel

TIMELINE OF EVENTS

1941: Mohammed Reza Pahlavi, known as the Shah, becomes the ruler of Iran.

1963: Rioting erupts as Ayatollah Khomeini preaches against the Shah. Khomeini is arrested.

1964: Khomeini is exiled, first to Turkey, then Iraq, and finally to France.

1965: Parvaneh (Pari) and Maheen Hakimian are born in Tehran.

December, 1978: Six to nine million people — more than 10 percent of the country — march against the Shah throughout Iran.

January 17, 1979: The Shah flees Iran to Egypt, then Morocco, Mexico, and finally to the United States.

February 1, 1979: Ayatollah Khomeini arrives back in Iran in triumph from France.

February 11, 1979: The Shah's troops are overpowered and they surrender.

April 1, 1979: Iran is officially declared an Islamic republic.

November 4, 1979: U.S. Embassy hostage crisis — the U.S. Embassy building is overpowered and fifty-two American hostages are held for 444 days until January, 1981.

July, 1980: The former Shah dies of cancer in Egypt.

1983: The twins finish school and start working to save money for their escape.

August, 1987: Pari and Maheen escape to Israel via Pakistan.

GLOSSARY

Baba: Father

bazaar: a market of shops or stalls selling various goods

exit visas: papers that give someone permission to leave their home country and move somewhere else

fanatic: a person who is excited about something in a way that is extreme or not reasonable

gondhi: balls of ground chicken and chickpea flour, flavored with different spices

hijab: the traditional head covering worn by Muslim women

inshallah: God willing

Islamic regime: a government ruled by Islamic law

joon: dear

lavash: long, thin, flat Persian bread

Maman: Mother

nan-e-nochodchi: traditional Persian cookies made from chickpeas and pistachios

paan: bread

Rosh Hashanah: the Jewish New Year

Satmar chassidim: a Hassidic group originally from Hungary known for its generosity to other Jews

Shabbat: the Sabbath, also called "Shabbos"

sukkah: a booth with a roof of branches and leaves that is used during the Sukkot holiday

Sukkot: the Festival of Tabernacles, also called "Sukkos"

Tishah B'Av: a Jewish fast day commemorating the destruction of the Temples in Jerusalem

transit papers: papers that give someone permission to travel through a foreign country

ulpan: an Israeli school for learning Hebrew

Yom Kippur: a Jewish holiday observed with fasting and prayer

ABOUT THE AUTHOR

Shira Yehudit Djalilmand, originally from England, now lives in Tzfat with her husband and seven children. She has been a regular writer for *Mishpacha Jewish Family Weekly* for over a decade, and is also the author of several books, including *Yosef Chaim's World of Adventures — The Secret of the Ruined Castle* (for children), and her autobiography, *Rebel with a Cause* (Menucha Publishers, 2016). Shira Yehudit also works as a translator from Hebrew and has recently translated a biography of Rabbi Mordechai Eliyahu.

MORE GREAT BOOKS IN THE ESCAPE SERIES

ESCAPE TO SHANGHAI

RABBI NACHMAN SELTZER

Poland in the late 1930s has become a very dangerous place for Jews. Isaac Tzvi, a student in the Mir Yeshiva, knows he must escape. But the yeshiva's students and teachers must first get passports and visas to far-off places. Will they be able to flee Europe before the Nazis march in?

This is the true story of the Mir Yeshiva's survival against all odds. Readers will be fascinated to learn about the turbulent war years and the miraculous events that helped this famous yeshiva escape to Shanghai.

Available wherever Jewish books are sold or at www.menuchapublishers.com

MORE GREAT BOOKS IN THE ESCAPE SERIES

ESCAPE
FROM HURRICANE KATRINA

CHAYA SARA BEN SHACHAR

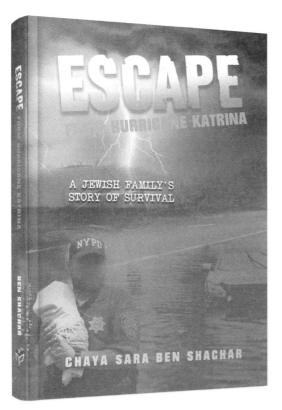

The city of New Orleans is in danger. A huge hurricane is on its way. The Rivkin family must decide whether to flee the city or to stay home. If they leave, will they be able to get out in time? Or will they be stuck in their car when the hurricane strikes? And what about all the people who are counting on their help?

This is the true story of a brave and compassionate family. Readers will be enthralled by this account of the day-to-day life of a Jewish family as it escapes from the aftermath of Hurricane Katrina.

MENUCHA PUBLISHERS

Available wherever Jewish books are sold or at www.menuchapublishers.com

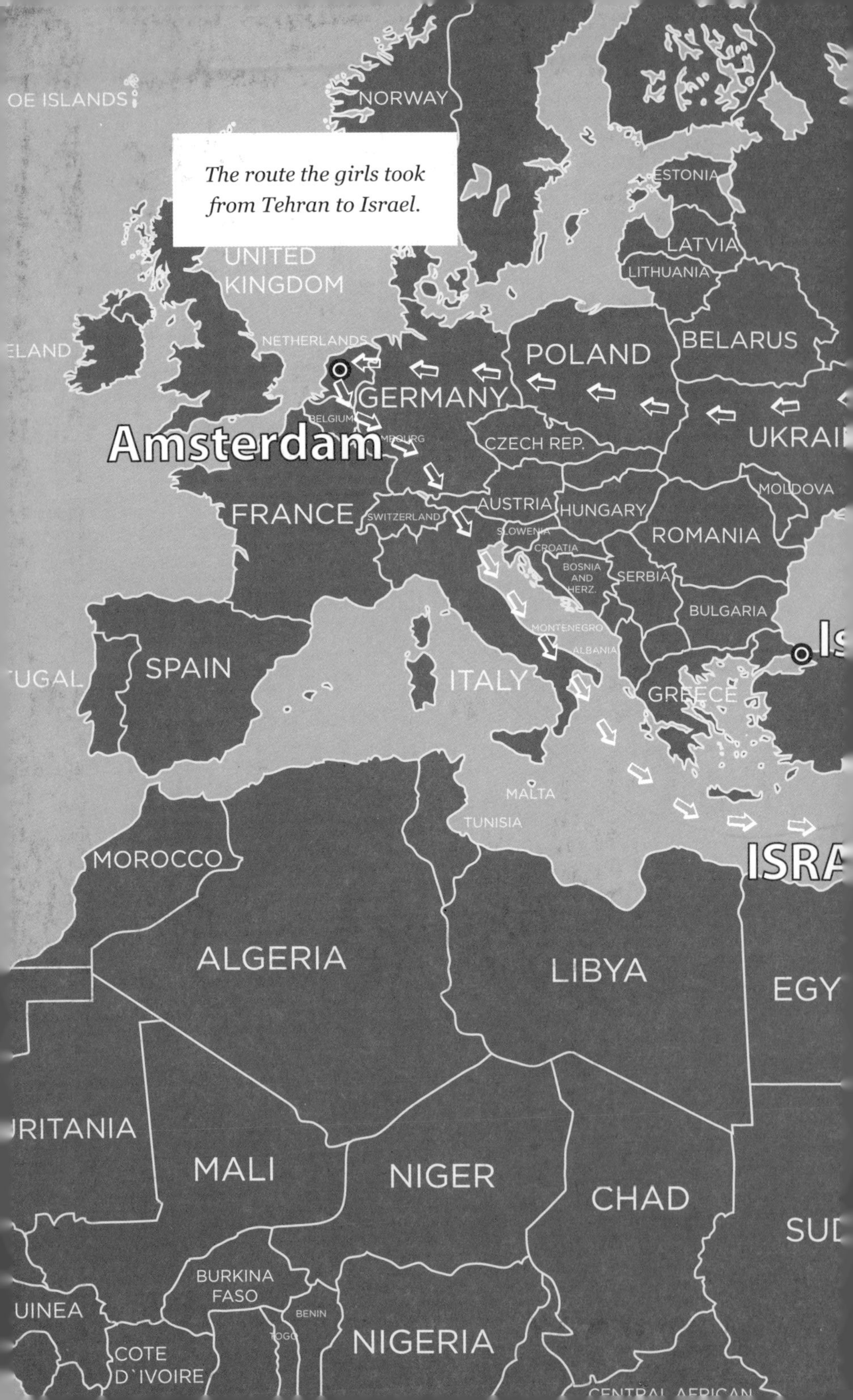

The route the girls took from Tehran to Israel.